I0430272

National Emergency Responder Credentialing

Emergency Medical Services Job Titles

FEMA 509-3

March 2008

 **FEMA**

Background	This document describes baseline and additional EMS criteria for the National Emergency Response Credentialing System.
Credentialing	The EMS Working Group determined the job titles listed herein to be the most commonly requested EMS personnel in a state-to-state, mutual aid-based response.
1. Required Criteria	Considering existing, nationally-accepted standards and/guidelines, the EMS Working Group extracted relevant education, training, experience, physical/medical fitness, certification, and licensing criteria to define the baseline criteria for each job title listed. These baseline criteria represent the minimum requirements for EMS personnel to participate in the Incident Management Integration Systems Division's National Emergency Responder Credentialing System.
2. Recommended Criteria	The EMS Working Group identified additional recommended criteria relating to education, training, certification, experience, and physical/medical fitness where it believed such standards and baseline criteria might enhance job performance. These criteria are not required and represent the EMS Working Group's recommendations for EMS personnel to participate in the Incident Management Systems Integration Division's Emergency Responder Credentialing System.
3. Clinically-based courses	Many nationally recognized clinically-based certification/verification courses such as Advanced Cardiac Life Support are appropriate and essential resources for field personnel. Such courses are not included within these criteria because they are recognized as an employer/system expectation commonly used to measure knowledge and performance. They are desirable but have not been included within these criteria as a requirement that must be inventoried.
4. Equivalent Courses	Per NIMS compliance at the time of publication, ICS- and IS- training courses are listed. Equivalent courses must meet the NIMS Five-Year Training Plan. As NIMS compliance requirements change, the requirements in this document will change to match them.
5. Categories	Please refer to the Definitions section for the categories used in the National Emergency Responder Credentialing System.
Website	For more information, you can also refer to the National Integration Center Incident Management Integration Systems Division "Resource Management" web site located at: http://www.fema.gov/emergency/nims/ResourceMngmnt.shtm#item1

Acronyms / Definitions

AEMT	Advanced Emergency Medical Technician
AHJ	Authority Having Jurisdiction
ATP	Airline Transport Pilot
CAMTS	Commission on Accreditation of Medical Transport Systems
CBRNE	Chemical, biological, radiological, nuclear, and high-yield explosives
Certification	Designation granted by AHJ that an individual has met requirements and achieved specific knowledge, skills, and abilities
CEVO	Emergency Vehicle Operator's Course
DDC4	Defensive Driving Course (4 hour course)
DEA	Drug Enforcement Administration
Education	Formal instruction based on a curriculum that prepares an individual with the core knowledge and skill for entry into a discipline and for performing a job function
EMR	Emergency Medical Responder
EMS	Emergency Medical Services
EMT	Emergency Medical Technician
EVO	Emergency Vehicle Operator
Experience	Time required functioning in a job title for an individual to attain proficiency in applying knowledge, skills, and abilities
FAA	Federal Aviation Administration
FEMA	Federal Emergency Management Agency
GVW	Gross Vehicle Weight
HazMat	Hazardous Materials
ICS	Incident Command System
IS	Independent Study
Licensing	Legal designation granted by AHJ that an individual has met the necessary legal requirements to function in a job title
MCI	Mass Casualty Incident
NHTSA	National Highway Transportation Safety Administration
NIMS	National Incident Management System
NREMT	National Registry of Emergency Medical Technicians
NRF	National Response Framework
NRP	Neonatal Resuscitation Program
OSHA	Occupational Safety and Health Administration
Physical/Medical Fitness	Physical and medical considerations that when applied, help to ensure safe performance in risky environments.
PIC	Pilot in Command
Single Resource	Personnel and major items of equipment, supplies, and facilities available or potentially available for assignment to incident operations and for which status is maintained.
Td	Tetanus and Diphtheria
Tdap	Tetanus, Diphtheria, and Pertussis
Training	Instruction and/or activities that enhance an individual's core knowledge, increase a skill set and proficiency, and strengthen and augment abilities.
VFR	Visual Flight Rules

 FEMA

Table of Contents
Credentialing EMS Titles

1. Advanced Emergency Medical Technician

DESCRIPTION:	The primary focus of the Advanced Emergency Medical Technician (AEMT) is to provide triage, assessment and limited advanced emergency medical care, under medical oversight. This may occur at an emergency scene until transportation resources arrive, during triage, from an emergency scene to a health care facility, or between health care facilities.
	The AEMT possesses the education and experience in areas of patient care that are commensurate with the patient care mission, provides care to minimize secondary injury and provides comfort to the patient and family while transporting the patient to an emergency care facility.
	The major difference between the Advanced Emergency Medical Technician and the Emergency Medical Technician is the AEMT's ability to perform limited advanced skills and pharmacological interventions.

Table 1-1: Required Criteria

EDUCATION:	Completion of a state-approved Advanced EMT program.

TRAINING:
SEE NOTE 1
	Completion of the following courses/curricula:
	1. ICS-100: Introduction to ICS.
	2. IS-700.A: NIMS, An Introduction.
	3. IS-800.B: NRF, An Introduction.
	4. HazMat Awareness Training or equivalent basic instruction consistent with:
	    a. the hazards anticipated to be present, or present at the scene
	    b. the probable impact of those hazards, based upon the mission role of the individual
	    c. use of the personal protective equipment consistent with "Guidance on Emergency Responder Personal Protective Equipment (PPE) for Response to CBRN Terrorism Incidents," Dept of HHS, Centers for Disease Control and Prevention, National Institute for Occupational Safety and Health (June 2008).

EXPERIENCE:	Ongoing, active participation as an AEMT with an EMS-providing entity, organization, or agency as an AEMT.
CERTIFICATION:	Successful completion of a state-approved program at this level or NREMT certification at this level.
LICENSING:	Active status of legal authority to function as an Advanced Emergency Medical Technician granted by a state, the District of Columbia, or U.S. territory.

COMMENTS:	**Note 1:** Per NIMS compliance at the time of publication, ICS- and FEMA IS- training courses are listed. Equivalent courses must meet the NIMS Five-Year Training Plan. As NIMS compliance requirements change, the requirements in this document will change to match them. **Note 2:** The personnel descriptions contained in this document are based upon the guidelines contained in the National EMS Scope of Practice Model document, which can be found at www.ems.gov.

Table 1-2: Recommended Criteria

EDUCATION:	Successful completion of the minimum terminal learning objectives for Advanced EMT as defined by NHTSA National EMS Education Standards. See Note 1.
TRAINING:	Completion of the following courses/curricula: 1. ICS-200: Basic ICS. 2. Ongoing training in the management and care of patients involved in an MCI.

PHYSICAL/ MEDICAL FITNESS:	1. Individuals must be healthy enough to function under field conditions, which may include some or all of the following:
	   • 12-hour shifts, austere conditions (possibly no showers, housing in tents, portable toilets).
	   • Extreme weather conditions (long exposure to heat and humidity, lack of air conditioning, extreme cold, wet environments).
	   • Long periods of standing.
	2. Individuals should not require personal medications that need refrigeration.
	3. Individuals should not have any physical conditions, impairments, or restrictions that would preclude them from participating in the moving and lifting or patients and/or equipment and supplies.
	4. Immunizations:
	Refer to immunization recommendations for emergency responders by Centers for Disease Control.
	   • Td toxoid or Tdap. Receipt of primary series and booster within the past 10 years.
	   • Completion of Hepatitis B Vaccination Series OR completion of a waiver of liability.

COMMENTS:	**Note 1:** NHTSA National EMS Education Standards are a component of the EMS Education Agenda for the Future: A System Approach, a comprehensive plan for a national EMS education system. The State equivalent to EMRs, EMTs, Advanced EMTs and paramedics are anticipated to transition to these educational standards as they are implemented.

2. Air Medical Transport Manager or Administrator	
DESCRIPTION:	The primary focus of an Air Medical Transport Manager or Administrator is patient and air medical crew safety through the coordination of patient transportation and the maintenance of records relating to patient identification, condition, and destination via rotary-wing or fixed-wing ambulance. The Air Medical Transport Manager: 1. Assists in the identification and allocation of resources to support all air missions. 2. May facilitate the communication of information between the scene and sending/receiving facilities in conjunction with the Air Medical Transport Physician. 3. Coordinates aviation with the Aviation Coordinator, Air Operations Branch Director, and other transportation team leaders.

Table 2-1: Required Criteria

TRAINING:
SEE NOTE 1
	Completion of the following courses/curricula:
	
	1. ICS-100: Introduction to ICS.
	
	2. ICS-200: Basic ICS.
	
	3. IS-700.A: NIMS, An Introduction.
	
	4. IS-800.B: NRF, An Introduction.
	
	5. HazMat Awareness Training or equivalent basic instruction consistent with:
	
	   a. the hazards anticipated to be present, or present at the scene
	
	   b. the probable impact of those hazards, based upon the mission role of the individual
	
	   c. use of the personal protective equipment consistent with "Guidance on Emergency Responder Personal Protective Equipment (PPE) for Response to CBRN Terrorism Incidents," Dept of HHS, Centers for Disease Control and Prevention, National Institute for Occupational Safety and Health (June 2008).

EXPERIENCE:	1. Minimum of 2 years supervisory, management, or administrative experience with an air medical transport service. 2. Knowledge of CAMTS accreditation and safety standards for patients requiring air medical transport.
COMMENTS:	**Note 1:** Per NIMS compliance at the time of publication, ICS and IS training courses are listed. Equivalent courses must meet the NIMS Five-Year Training Plan. As NIMS compliance requirements change, the requirements in this document will change to match them.

Table 2-2: Recommended Criteria

TRAINING:	Completion of the following courses/curricula: 1. Ongoing training in operations and management/care of patients involved in a MCI. 2. ICS-300: Intermediate ICS.
EXPERIENCE:	Medical Transport Leadership Institute or equivalent.

CERTIFICATION:	Certified Medical Transport Executive or equivalent college-level education.
PHYSICAL/ MEDICAL FITNESS:	1. Individuals must be healthy enough to function under field conditions, which may include some or all of the following: • 12-hour shifts, austere conditions (possibly no showers, housing in tents, portable toilets). • Extreme weather conditions (long exposure to heat and humidity, lack of air conditioning, extreme cold, wet environments). • Long periods of standing. 2. Individuals should not require personal medications that require refrigeration. 3. Individuals should not have any physical conditions, impairments, or restrictions that would preclude them from participating in the moving and lifting of patients and/or equipment and supplies. 5. Immunizations: Refer to immunization recommendations for emergency responders by Centers for Disease Control, including: • Td toxoid or Tdap. Receipt of primary series and booster within the past 10 years. • Completion of Hepatitis B Vaccination Series OR completion of a waiver of liability.

3. Air Medical Transport Mechanic	

DESCRIPTION:	The primary focus of the Air Medical Transport Mechanic is to ensure that aircraft used for medical missions are maintained at or above airworthiness standards prescribed by applicable regulations. The Air Medical Transport Mechanic:
	
	1. Is responsible for the direct operation and administration of avionics maintenance and support.
	2. Will ensure
	   • Compliance with FAA and other regulations.
	   • That aircraft avionics and avionics-related equipment inspection and maintenance records are originated and retained for review as needed.
	   • That specific equipment and special tools are made available to accomplish the inspections, maintenance, and repair or avionics-related components on any aircraft in use.
	   • That all appropriate entries have been made and/or transcribed to the aircraft journal and technical logs with respect to the avionics maintenance function and airworthiness status of the aircraft.

Table 3-1: Required Criteria

EDUCATION:	High school diploma or GED.
TRAINING:	Completion of FAA-certified mechanic school or equivalent on-the-job training.
CERTIFICATION:	Completion of Airframe and Powerplant Certification.
LICENSING:	Valid driver's license.

Table 3-2: Recommended Criteria

TRAINING:	1. HazMat Awareness Training or equivalent basic instruction consistent with:
	   a. the hazards anticipated to be present, or present at the scene
	   b. the probable impact of those hazards, based upon the mission role of the individual
	   c. use of the personal protective equipment consistent with "Guidance on Emergency Responder Personal Protective Equipment (PPE) for Response to CBRN Terrorism Incidents," Dept of HHS, Centers for Disease Control and Prevention, National Institute for Occupational Safety and Health (June 2008).

EXPERIENCE:	Minimum of 2 years experience working as an aviation mechanic.

PHYSICAL/ MEDICAL FITNESS:	1. Individuals must be healthy enough to function under field conditions, which may include some or all of the following: • 12-hour shifts, austere conditions (possibly no showers, housing in tents, portable toilets). • Extreme weather conditions (long exposure to heat and humidity, lack of air conditioning, extreme cold, wet environments). • Long periods of standing. 2. Individuals should not require personal medications that require refrigeration. 3. Individuals should not have any physical conditions, impairments, or restrictions that would preclude them from participating in the moving and lifting of patients and/or equipment and supplies. 4. Immunizations: Refer to immunization recommendations for emergency responders by Centers for Disease Control, including: • Td toxoid or Tdap. Receipt of primary series and booster within the past 10 years. • Completion of Hepatitis B Vaccination Series OR completion of a waiver of liability.

4. Air Medical Transport Paramedic	
DESCRIPTION:	The primary focus of the Air Medical Transport Paramedic is the acute management and transportation of the broad range of patients who access the emergency medical system. The Air Medical Transport Paramedic: 1. Possesses the basic and advanced skills to include invasive and pharmacological interventions to reduce the morbidity and mortality associated with acute out-of-hospital medical and traumatic emergencies. Emergency care is based on an advanced assessment and the formulation of a field impression. 2. Has education and experience in areas of patient care commensurate with the patient care mission. 3. May be called upon to assist in the triage of patients and provides care designed to minimize secondary injury and provide comfort to the patient and family while transporting the patient to an appropriate health care facility.

Table 4-1: Required Criteria

EDUCATION:	Completion of a state-approved paramedic program based on the NHTSA National Standard Curriculum.

TRAINING:
 SEE NOTE 1
	Completion of the following courses/curricula:
	
	 1. ICS-100: Introduction to ICS.
	 2. ICS-200: Basic ICS.
	 3. IS-700.A: NIMS, An Introduction.
	 4. IS-800.B: NRF, An Introduction.
	 5. HazMat Awareness Training or equivalent basic instruction consistent with:
	
	    a. the hazards anticipated to be present, or present at the scene
	    b. the probable impact of those hazards, based upon the mission role of the individual
	    c. use of the personal protective equipment consistent with "Guidance on Emergency Responder Personal Protective Equipment (PPE) for Response to CBRN Terrorism Incidents," Dept of HHS, Centers for Disease Control and Prevention, National Institute for Occupational Safety and Health (June 2008).

EXPERIENCE:	Ongoing, active participation with an air medical transport service.
CERTIFICATION:	Successful completion of a state-approved program at this level or NREMT certification at this level.
LICENSING:	Active status of legal authority to function as a paramedic granted by a state, the District of Columbia, or U.S. territory.

COMMENTS:	**Note 1:** Per NIMS compliance at the time of publication, ICS and IS training courses are listed. Equivalent courses must meet the NIMS Five-Year Training Plan. As NIMS compliance requirements change, the requirements in this document will change to match them.
	Note 2: The personnel descriptions contained in this document are based upon the guidelines contained in the National EMS Scope of Practice Model document, which can be found at www.ems.gov.

Table 4-2: Recommended Criteria

EDUCATION:	Successful completion of the minimum terminal learning objectives for Paramedic as defined by NHTSA National EMS Education Standards. See Note 1.
TRAINING:	Completion of the following courses/curricula: 1. Ongoing training in the management and care of patients involved in an MCI. 2. Neonatal Resuscitation Program (NRP) or equivalent, if expected to transport high-risk OB or neonatal patients.
EXPERIENCE:	1. Minimum of 2 years of emergency and critical care paramedic experience. 2. Knowledge of CAMTS Accreditation Standards for patients requiring air medical transport.
CERTIFICATION:	Certified Flight Paramedic (FP-C)

PHYSICAL/ MEDICAL FITNESS:	1. Individuals must be healthy enough to function under field conditions, which may include some or all of the following:
	  • 12-hour shifts, austere conditions (possibly no showers, housing in tents, portable toilets).
	  • Extreme weather conditions (long exposure to heat and humidity, lack of air conditioning, extreme cold, wet environments).
	  • Long periods of standing.
	2. Individuals should not require personal medications that require refrigeration.
	3. Individuals should not have any physical conditions, impairments, or restrictions that would preclude them from participating in the moving and lifting of patients and/or equipment and supplies.
	4. Immunizations:
	Refer to immunization recommendations for emergency responders by Centers for Disease Control, including:
	  • Td toxoid or Tdap. Receipt of primary series and booster within the past 10 years.
	  • Completion of Hepatitis B Vaccination Series OR completion of a waiver of liability.

COMMENTS:	**Note 1:** NHTSA National EMS Education Standards are a component of the EMS Education Agenda for the Future: A System Approach, a comprehensive plan for a national EMS education system. The State equivalent to EMRs, EMTs, Advanced EMTs and paramedics are anticipated to transition to these educational standards as they are implemented.

5. Air Medical Transport Physician	
DESCRIPTION:	The primary purpose of the Air Medical Transport Physician is to oversee the care that the air medical transport crew delivers to the patient from the point of initial contact throughout the entire transport and appropriate deposition of the patient to the point of definitive care. The Air Medical Transport Physician: 1. Is a licensed physician with education and experience in the areas of medicine and pre-hospital care commensurate with the patient care mission. 2. Serves as a clinical resource to the air medical transport crew. 3. Has the authority over all patient care and clinical aspects of the air medical transport service.

Table 5-1: Required Criteria

EDUCATION:	Graduate of an accredited medical school and completion of an accredited residency program.

TRAINING:
SEE NOTE 1
	Completion of the following courses/curricula:
	1. ICS-100: Introduction to ICS.
	2. ICS-200: Basic ICS.
	3. IS-700.A: NIMS, An Introduction.
	4. IS-800.B: NRF, An Introduction.
	5. HazMat Awareness Training or equivalent basic instruction consistent with:
	    a. the hazards anticipated to be present, or present at the scene
	    b. the probable impact of those hazards, based upon the mission role of the individual
	    c. use of the personal protective equipment consistent with "Guidance on Emergency Responder Personal Protective Equipment (PPE) for Response to CBRN Terrorism Incidents," Dept of HHS, Centers for Disease Control and Prevention, National Institute for Occupational Safety and Health (June 2008).
	6. Air Medical Physician Association's (AMPA) Medical Director Core Curriculum or equivalent basic training as an aviation medical transport (AMT) medical director.

EXPERIENCE:	Ongoing, active participation with an established air medical transport service.
CERTIFICATION:	Completion of the following: 1. Board certification or board-eligible in emergency medicine (or comparable specialty). 2. Current DEA Registration.
LICENSING:	Active status of legal authority to function as a physician granted by a state, the District of Columbia, or U.S. territory.
COMMENTS:	**Note 1:** Per NIMS compliance at the time of publication, ICS and IS training courses are listed. Equivalent courses must meet the NIMS Five-Year Training Plan. As NIMS compliance requirements change, the requirements in this document will change to match them.

Table 5-2: Recommended Criteria

TRAINING:	Completion of the following courses/curricula: 1. ICS-300: Intermediate ICS. 2. Base Station Course or equivalent.
EXPERIENCE:	1. Active participation in the care of critically ill/injured patients. 2. Knowledge of CAMTS Accreditation Standards for patients requiring air medical transport.
PHYSICAL/ MEDICAL FITNESS:	1. Individuals must be healthy enough to function under field conditions, which may include some or all of the following: • 12-hour shifts, austere conditions (possibly no showers, housing in tents, portable toilets). • Extreme weather conditions (long exposure to heat and humidity, lack of air conditioning, extreme cold, wet environments). • Long periods of standing. 2. Individuals should not require personal medications that require refrigeration. 3. Individuals should not have any physical conditions, impairments, or restrictions that would preclude them from participating in the moving and lifting of patients and/or equipment and supplies. 4. Immunizations: Refer to immunization recommendations for emergency responders by Centers for Disease Control, including: • Td toxoid or Tdap. Receipt of primary series and booster within the past 10 years. • Completion of Hepatitis B Vaccination Series OR completion of a waiver of liability.

6. Air Medical Transport Pilot (Rotorcraft)	
DESCRIPTION:	The primary focus of the Air Medical Transport Pilot is the safe, coordinated transport of air medical personnel and equipment to the location of patients and subsequent provision of safe, coordinated transport of patients to an appropriate destination. The Air Medical Transport Pilot (Rotorcraft) has authority for acceptance of specific missions and will make all decisions concerning suitability of weather conditions, landing areas, condition of the aircraft for flight, loading of the aircraft, and other factors affecting flight safety.

Table 6-1: Required Criteria

EDUCATION:	Completion of required ground school on aeronautical knowledge; pass the required knowledge and practical test that apply to the aircraft type and class certificate sought.

TRAINING:
SEE NOTE 1
	Completion of the following courses/criteria:
	1. ICS-100: Introduction to ICS.
	2. ICS-200: Basic ICS.
	3. IS-700.A: NIMS, An Introduction.
	4. HazMat Awareness Training or equivalent basic instruction consistent with:
	    a. the hazards anticipated to be present, or present at the scene
	    b. the probable impact of those hazards, based upon the mission role of the individual
	    c. use of the personal protective equipment consistent with "Guidance on Emergency Responder Personal Protective Equipment (PPE) for Response to CBRN Terrorism Incidents," Dept of HHS, Centers for Disease Control and Prevention, National Institute for Occupational Safety and Health (June 2008).
	5. Risk assessment training and hazard mitigation.
	6. Air Medical Resource Management/Aeronautical Decision Making (ADM)/Crew Resource Management.

EXPERIENCE:	Pilot is current in aircraft type and pilot rating as determined by the AHJ. Completion of the following: 1. 2000 hours of pilot-in-command time (in helicopters for rotorcraft operations). 2. 250 hours of unaided night time. 3. 300 hours of turbine time. 4. 100 hours of EMS time.
PHYSICAL/MEDIC AL FITNESS:	Annual flight physical with medical class certificate that corresponds with the pilot certificate/rating.
CERTIFICATION:	Completion of one of the following: 1. Commercial Pilot Certificate with Instrument Rating. See Note 2. 2. Military or Public Use pilot equivalent training, documented to the same standard or higher.

COMMENTS:	**Note 1:** Per NIMS compliance at the time of publication, ICS and IS training courses are listed. Equivalent courses must meet the NIMS Five-Year Training Plan. As NIMS compliance requirements change, the requirements in this document will change to match them. **Note 2:** The Commercial Pilot Certificate/Instrument Rating need not be current.

Table 6-2: Recommended Criteria

TRAINING:	1. Ongoing training in operations of management and care of patients involved in MCI incidents. 2. 100 hours night-vision goggles. 3. Hoist operations, rappelling operations, mountain operations, desert operations, and over-water operations as applicable to the mission the pilot will be asked to perform.
PHYSICAL/ MEDICAL FITNESS:	1. Individuals must be healthy enough to function under field conditions, which may include some or all of the following: <ul><li>12-hour shifts, austere conditions (possibly no showers, housing in tents, portable toilets).</li><li>Extreme weather conditions (long exposure to heat and humidity, lack of air conditioning, extreme cold, wet environments).</li><li>Long periods of standing.</li></ul>2. Individuals should not require personal medications that require refrigeration. 3. Individuals should not have any physical conditions, impairments, or restrictions that would preclude them from participating in the moving and lifting of patients and/or equipment and supplies. 4. Immunizations: Refer to immunization recommendations for emergency responders by Centers for Disease Control, including: <ul><li>Td toxoid or Tdap. Receipt of primary series and booster within the past 10 years.</li><li>Completion of Hepatitis B Vaccination Series OR completion of a waiver of liability.</li></ul>

7. Air Medical Transport Registered Nurse	
DESCRIPTION:	The primary focus of the Air Medical Transport Registered Nurse is to provide direct care and transportation of critical and emergent patients who access the EMS scene or inter-facility health care system. The Air Medical Transport Registered Nurse possesses the education and experience in areas of patient care commensurate with the patient care mission, and will serve as a functional member of the air medical transport crew, providing critical assessment, triage, treatment, and transportation of patient via rotor-wing or fixed-wing ambulance.

Table7-1: Required Criteria

EDUCATION:	Graduate of an accredited nursing program.
TRAINING: SEE NOTE 1	Completion of the following courses/curricula: 1. ICS-100: Introduction to ICS. 2. ICS-200: Basic ICS. 3. IS-700.A: NIMS, An Introduction. 4. IS-800.B: NRF, An Introduction. 5. HazMat Awareness Training or equivalent basic instruction consistent with: a. the hazards anticipated to be present, or present at the scene b. the probable impact of those hazards, based upon the mission role of the individual c. use of the personal protective equipment consistent with "Guidance on Emergency Responder Personal Protective Equipment (PPE) for Response to CBRN Terrorism Incidents," Dept of HHS, Centers for Disease Control and Prevention, National Institute for Occupational Safety and Health (June 2008).
EXPERIENCE:	Ongoing, active participation with an established air medical transport service.
LICENSING:	Active status of legal authority to function as a registered nurse granted by a state, the District of Columbia, or U.S. territory.
COMMENTS:	**Note 1:** Per NIMS compliance at the time of publication, ICS and IS training courses are listed. Equivalent courses must meet the NIMS Five-Year Training Plan. As NIMS compliance requirements change, the requirements in this document will change to match them.

Table 7-2: Recommended Criteria

TRAINING:	Completion of the following courses/curricula: 1. Ongoing training in the management of patients involved in a MCI. 2. Neonatal Resuscitation Program (NRP) or equivalent, if expected to transport high risk OB or neonatal patients.
EXPERIENCE:	1. Minimum of 2 years of emergency and critical care nursing experience. 2. Knowledge of CAMTS Accreditation Standards for patients requiring air medical transport.

CERTIFICATION:	Completion of at least one of the following:
	• Certified Flight Registered Nurse (CFRN).
	• Certified Transport Registered Nurse (CTRN).
	• Certified Emergency Nurse (CEN).
	• Critical Care Registered Nurse (CCRN).
PHYSICAL/ MEDICAL FITNESS:	1. Individuals must be healthy enough to function under field conditions, which may include some or all of the following:
	• 12-hour shifts, austere conditions (possibly no showers, housing in tents, portable toilets).
	• Extreme weather conditions (long exposure to heat and humidity, lack of air conditioning, extreme cold, wet environments).
	• Long periods of standing.
	2. Individuals should not require personal medications that require refrigeration.
	3. Individuals should not have any physical conditions, impairments, or restrictions that would preclude them from participating in the moving and lifting of patients and/or equipment and supplies.
	4. Immunizations:
	Refer to immunization recommendations for emergency responders by Centers for Disease Control, including:
	• Td toxoid or Tdap. Receipt of primary series and booster within the past 10 years.
	• Completion of Hepatitis B Vaccination Series OR completion of a waiver of liability.

8. Ambulance Strike Team / Ambulance Task Force Leader	
DESCRIPTION:	The primary focus of the Ambulance Strike Team Leader is to provide direct supervision and guidance to a group of EMS personnel, functioning as ambulance crews, who are able to respond as a deployable resource in a strike team configuration. The Ambulance Strike Team Leader is responsible for supervising tactical assignments assigned to the Strike Team. The Leader reports work progress and status of resources, maintains work records on assigned personnel, and relays other important information to their supervisor An Ambulance Strike Team / Ambulance Task Force Leader: 1. Reviews Common Responsibilities with crews. 2. Reviews assignments with subordinates and assign tasks. 3. Monitors work progress and makes changes when necessary. 4. Coordinates activities with other strike teams, task forces and single resources. 5. Travels to and from active assignment areas with assigned resources. 6. Retains control of assigned resources while in available or out-of-service status. 7. Submits situation and resource status information to Division/Group Supervisor. 8. Maintains Unit/Activity Log.

Table 8-1: Required Criteria

EDUCATION:	Completion of a state-approved EMT or paramedic program based on NHTSA National Standard Curriculum.

TRAINING:	Completion of the following courses / curricula:
	
	1. ICS-100: Introduction to ICS.
	2. ICS-200: Basic ICS.
	3. ICS-300: Intermediate ICS.
	4. IS-700.A: NIMS, An Introduction.
	5. IS-800.B: NRF, An Introduction.
	6. HazMat Awareness Training or equivalent basic instruction consistent with:
	    a. the hazards anticipated to be present, or present at the scene
	    b. the probable impact of those hazards, based upon the mission role of the individual
	    c. use of the personal protective equipment consistent with "Guidance on Emergency Responder Personal Protective Equipment (PPE) for Response to CBRN Terrorism Incidents," Dept of HHS, Centers for Disease Control and Prevention, National Institute for Occupational Safety and Health (June 2008).
	7. State-recognized Ambulance Strike Team Leader or Ambulance Task Force Leader Training Course.

EXPERIENCE:	1. 3 years of EMS experience. 2. 1 year of leadership experience in EMS or related field. 3. Ongoing, active participation with an EMS providing entity, organization, or agency.
CERTIFICATION:	Successful completion of a state-approved or state-recognized Ambulance Strike Team Leader/Medical Task Force Leader program.
LICENSING:	Active status of legal authority to function as an Emergency Medical Technician or Paramedic granted by a state, the District of Columbia, or U.S. territory.
COMMENTS:	**Note 1:** Per NIMS compliance at the time of publication, ICS- and FEMA IS- training courses are listed. Equivalent courses must meet the NIMS Five-Year Training Plan. As NIMS compliance requirements change, the requirements in this document will change to match them. Presently, the training for a Strike Team Leader is not widely available or standardized. The individual filling this assignment must be authorized to do so by the deploying state, the District of Columbia, or U.S. territory.

Table 8-2: Recommended Criteria

EDUCATION:	Successful completion of a state-approved paramedic program based on NHTSA National Standard Curriculum.
PHYSICAL/ MEDICAL FITNESS:	1. Individuals must be healthy enough to function under field conditions, which may include all or some of the following: • 12-hour shifts, austere conditions (possibly no showers, housing in tents, portable toilets). • Extreme weather conditions (long exposure to heat and humidity, lack of air conditioning, extreme cold, or wet environments). • Long periods of standing or sitting. 2. Individuals should not require personal medications that need refrigeration. 3. Individuals should not have any physical conditions, impairments, or restrictions that would preclude them from participating in the moving and lifting of patients and/or equipment and supplies. 4. Immunizations: Refer to immunization recommendations for emergency responders by Centers for Disease Control, including: • Td toxoid or Tdap. Receipt of primary series and booster within the past 10 years. • Completion of Hepatitis B Vaccination Series OR completion of a waiver of liability.

9. Emergency Medical Responder	
DESCRIPTION:	The primary focus of the Emergency Medical Responder (EMR) is to initiate immediate lifesaving care to patients who access the emergency medical system. The Emergency Medical Responder possesses education and experience in areas of patient care commensurate with the patient care mission. Additionally, the EMR: 1. Has the basic knowledge and skills necessary to provide lifesaving interventions while awaiting additional EMS response and to assist higher level personnel at the scene and during transport. 2. Functions as part of a comprehensive EMS response, under medical oversight. 3. Performs initial triage and basic interventions with minimal equipment.

Table 9-1: Required Criteria

EDUCATION:	Completion of state-approved first responder program based on the NHTSA National Standard Curriculum.

TRAINING:
SEE NOTE 1
	Completion of the following courses/curricula:
	
	1. ICS-100: Introduction to ICS.
	2. IS-700.A: NIMS, An Introduction.
	3. HazMat Awareness Training or equivalent basic instruction consistent with:
	   a. the hazards anticipated to be present, or present at the scene
	   b. the probable impact of those hazards, based upon the mission role of the individual
	   c. use of the personal protective equipment consistent with "Guidance on Emergency Responder Personal Protective Equipment (PPE) for Response to CBRN Terrorism Incidents," Dept of HHS, Centers for Disease Control and Prevention, National Institute for Occupational Safety and Health (June 2008).

EXPERIENCE:	Ongoing, active participation with an EMS-providing entity, organization, or agency.
CERTIFICATION:	Successful completion of a state-approved program at this level or NREMT certification at this level.
LICENSING:	Active status of legal authority to function as a First Responder or an Emergency Medical Responder granted by a state, the District of Columbia, or U.S. territory.
COMMENTS:	**Note 1:** Per NIMS compliance at the time of publication, ICS and IS training courses are listed. Equivalent courses must meet the NIMS Five-Year Training Plan. As NIMS compliance requirements change, the requirements in this document will change to match them. **Note 2:** The personnel descriptions contained in this document are based upon the guidelines contained in the National EMS Scope of Practice Model document, which can be found at www.ems.gov.

Table 9-2: Recommended Criteria

EDUCATION:	Successful completion of the minimum terminal learning objectives for Emergency Medical Responder as defined by the NHTSA National EMS Education Standard. See Note 1.
TRAINING:	1. Ongoing training in the management and care of patients involved in an MCI. 2. ICS-200: Basic ICS.

PHYSICAL/ MEDICAL FITNESS:	1. Individuals must be healthy enough to function under field conditions, which may include some or all of the following:
	   • 12-hour shifts, austere conditions (possibly no showers, housing in tents, portable toilets).
	   • Extreme weather conditions (long exposure to heat and humidity, lack of air conditioning, extreme cold, wet environments).
	   • Long periods of standing.
	2. Individuals should not require personal medications that require refrigeration.
	3. Individuals should not have any physical conditions, impairments, or restrictions that would preclude them from participating in the moving and lifting of patients and/or equipment and supplies.
	4. Immunizations:
	Refer to immunization recommendations for emergency responders by Centers for Disease Control, including:
	   • Td toxoid or Tdap. Receipt of primary series and booster within the past 10 years.
	   • Completion of Hepatitis B Vaccination Series OR completion of a waiver of liability.

COMMENTS:	**Note 1:** NHTSA National EMS Education Standards are a component of the EMS Education Agenda for the Future: A System Approach, a comprehensive plan for a national EMS education system. The State equivalent EMRs, EMTs, Advanced EMTs and paramedics are expected to transition to these educational standards as they are implemented. Presently, many states use the title of "First Responder' to indicate an EMR.

10. Emergency Medical Task Force Leader

DESCRIPTION:	The primary focus of the Emergency Medical Task Force Leader is to provide direct supervision and guidance to a group of EMS personnel, functioning as crews, who are able to respond as a deployable resource in a task force team configuration
	The Emergency Medical Task Force Leader is responsible for supervising tactical assignments assigned to the Emergency Medical Task Force. The Leader reports work progress and status of resources, maintains work records on assigned personnel, and relays other important information to the supervisor.
	An Emergency Medical Task Force Leader:
	1. Reviews Common Responsibilities with crew supervisors.
	2. Reviews assignments with subordinates and assign tasks.
	3. Monitors work progress and makes changes when necessary.
	4. Coordinates activities with other strike teams, task forces and single resources.
	5. Travels to and from active assignment areas with assigned resources.
	6. Retains control of assigned resources while in available or out-of-service status.
	7. Submits situation and resource status information to Division/Group Supervisor.
	8. Maintains Unit/Activity Log.

Table 10-1: Required Criteria

EDUCATION:	Completion of a state-approved EMT or paramedic program based on NHTSA National Standard Curriculum.
TRAINING:	Completion of the following courses / curricula:
	1. ICS-100: Introduction to ICS.
	2. ICS-200: Basic ICS.
	3. ICS-300: Intermediate ICS.
	4. IS-700.A: NIMS, An Introduction.
	5. IS-800.B: NRF, An Introduction.
	6. HazMat Awareness Training or equivalent basic instruction consistent with:
	a. the hazards anticipated to be present, or present at the scene
	b. the probable impact of those hazards, based upon the mission role of the individual
	c. use of the personal protective equipment consistent with "Guidance on Emergency Responder Personal Protective Equipment (PPE) for Response to CBRN Terrorism Incidents," Dept of HHS, Centers for Disease Control and Prevention, National Institute for Occupational Safety and Health (June 2008).
	7. State approved or state-recognized Emergency Medical Task Force Leader Training Course.

EXPERIENCE:	1. 3 years of EMS experience.
	2. 1 year of leadership experience in EMS or related field.
	3. Ongoing, active participation with an EMS providing entity, organization, or agency.
CERTIFICATION:	Successful completion of a state-approved or state-recognized Ambulance Strike Team Leader/Medical Task Force Leader program.
LICENSING:	Active status of legal authority to function as an Emergency Medical Technician or Paramedic granted by a state, the District of Columbia, or U.S. territory.
COMMENTS:	**Note 1:** Per NIMS compliance at the time of publication, ICS- and FEMA IS- training courses are listed. Equivalent courses must meet the NIMS Five-Year Training Plan. As NIMS compliance requirements change, the requirements in this document will change to match them. Presently, the training for a Task Force Leader is not widely available or standardized. The individual filling this assignment must be authorized to do so by the deploying state, the District of Columbia, or U.S. territory.

Table 10-2: Recommended Criteria

PHYSICAL/ MEDICAL FITNESS:	1. Individuals must be healthy enough to function under field conditions, which may include all or some of the following: • 12-hour shifts, austere conditions (possibly no showers, housing in tents, portable toilets). • Extreme weather conditions (long exposure to heat and humidity, lack of air conditioning, extreme cold, or wet environments). • Long periods of standing or sitting. 2. Individuals should not require personal medications that need refrigeration. 3. Individuals should not have any physical conditions, impairments, or restrictions that would preclude them from participating in the moving and lifting of patients and/or equipment and supplies. 4. Immunizations: Refer to immunization recommendations for emergency responders by Centers for Disease Control, including: • Td toxoid or Tdap. Receipt of primary series and booster within the past 10 years. • Completion of Hepatitis B Vaccination Series OR completion of a waiver of liability.

11. Emergency Medical Technician

DESCRIPTION:	The primary focus of the Emergency Medical Technician (EMT) is to provide basic triage, assessment, and noninvasive interventions to reduce the morbidity and mortality associated with acute out-of-hospital medical and traumatic emergencies. This may occur at an emergency scene until transportation resources arrive, from an emergency scene to a health care facility or) between health care facilities.
	Additionally, the EMT possesses the education and experience in areas of patient care that are commensurate with the patient care mission, providing care to minimize secondary injury and provide comfort to the patient and family while transporting the patient to an emergency care facility. The EMT level is the minimum licensure level for personnel transporting patients in ambulances.

Table11-1: Required Criteria

EDUCATION:	Completion of a state-approved EMT program based on NHTSA National Standard Curriculum.

TRAINING:
SEE NOTE 1
	Completion of the following courses/curricula:
	
	1. ICS-100: Introduction to ICS.
	
	2. IS-700.A: NIMS, An Introduction.
	
	3. IS-800.B: NRF, An Introduction.
	
	4. HazMat Awareness Training or equivalent basic instruction consistent with:
	
	    a. the hazards anticipated to be present, or present at the scene
	
	    b. the probable impact of those hazards, based upon the mission role of the individual
	
	    c. use of the personal protective equipment consistent with "Guidance on Emergency Responder Personal Protective Equipment (PPE) for Response to CBRN Terrorism Incidents," Dept of HHS, Centers for Disease Control and Prevention, National Institute for Occupational Safety and Health (June 2008).

EXPERIENCE:	Ongoing, active participation with an EMS-providing entity, organization or agency.
CERTIFICATION:	Successful completion of a state-approved program at this level or NREMT certification at this level.
LICENSING:	Active status of legal authority to function as an Emergency Medical Technician granted by a state, the District of Columbia, or U.S. territory.
COMMENTS:	**Note 1:** Per NIMS compliance at the time of publication, ICS and IS training courses are listed. Equivalent courses must meet the NIMS Five-Year Training Plan. As NIMS compliance requirements change, the requirements in this document will change to match them. **Note 2:** The personnel descriptions contained in this document are based upon the guidelines contained in the National EMS Scope of Practice Model document, which can be found at www.ems.gov.

Table 11-2: Recommended Criteria

EDUCATION:	Successful completion of the minimum terminal learning objectives for EMT as defined by NHTSA National EMS Education Standards. See Note 1.
TRAINING:	Completion of the following courses/curricula: 1. ICS-200: Basic ICS. 2. Ongoing training in the management and care of patients involved in a MCI.
PHYSICAL/ MEDICAL FITNESS:	1. Individuals must be healthy enough to function under field conditions, which may include some or all of the following: • 12-hour shifts, austere conditions (possibly no showers, housing in tents, portable toilets). • Extreme weather conditions (long exposure to heat and humidity, lack of air conditioning, extreme cold, wet environments). • Long periods of standing. 2. Individuals should not require personal medications that require refrigeration. 3. Individuals should not have any physical conditions, impairments, or restrictions that would preclude them from participating in the moving and lifting of patients and/or equipment and supplies. 4. Immunizations: Refer to immunization recommendations for emergency responders by Centers for Disease Control, including: • Td toxoid or Tdap. Receipt of primary series and booster within the past 10 years. • Completion of Hepatitis B Vaccination Series OR completion of a waiver of liability.
COMMENTS:	**Note 1:** NHTSA National EMS Education Standards are a component of the EMS Education Agenda for the Future: A System Approach, a comprehensive plan for a national EMS education system. The State equivalent to EMRs, EMTs, Advanced EMTs and paramedics are expected to transition to these educational standards as they are implemented.

12. Emergency Vehicle Operator	
DESCRIPTION:	The primary focus of the Emergency Vehicle Operator (EVO) is the safe operation of assigned emergency vehicles less than 26,000 lbs GVW used for patient care and/or transport.

Table 12-1: Required Criteria

TRAINING: SEE NOTE 1	Completion of the following courses/curricula:
	1. ICS-100: Introduction to ICS.
	2. IS-700.A: NIMS, An Introduction.
	3. IS-800.B: NRF, An Introduction.
	4. HazMat Awareness Training or equivalent basic instruction consistent with:
	   a. the hazards anticipated to be present, or present at the scene
	   b. the probable impact of those hazards, based upon the mission role of the individual
	   c. use of the personal protective equipment consistent with "Guidance on Emergency Responder Personal Protective Equipment (PPE) for Response to CBRN Terrorism Incidents," Dept of HHS, Centers for Disease Control and Prevention, National Institute for Occupational Safety and Health (June 2008).
	5. CEVO or equivalent.
	6. DDC4 or equivalent.

EXPERIENCE:	Ongoing, active involvement with an EMS-providing entity, organization, or agency.
LICENSING:	Valid driver's license with appropriate endorsements if required by licensing state.
COMMENTS:	Note 1: Per NIMS compliance at the time of publication, ICS and IS training courses are listed. Equivalent courses must meet the NIMS Five-Year Training Plan. As NIMS compliance requirements change, the requirements in this document will change to match them.

Table 12-2: Recommended Criteria

EDUCATION:	2 years minimum driving experience plus a minimum of 1 year EVO experience.

PHYSICAL/ MEDICAL FITNESS:	1. Individuals must be healthy enough to function under field conditions, which may include some or all of the following:
	• 12-hour shifts, austere conditions (possibly no showers, housing in tents, portable toilets).
	• Extreme weather conditions (long exposure to heat and humidity, lack of air conditioning, extreme cold, wet environments).
	• Long periods of standing.
	2. Individuals should not require personal medications that require refrigeration.
	3. Individuals should not have any physical conditions, impairments, or restrictions that would preclude them from participating in the moving and lifting of patients and/or equipment and supplies.
	4. Immunizations:
	Refer to immunization recommendations for emergency responders by Centers for Disease Control, including:
	• Td toxoid or Tdap. Receipt of primary series and booster within the past 10 years.
	• Completion of Hepatitis B Vaccination Series OR completion of a waiver of liability.

13. Emergency Vehicle Operator- Heavy

DESCRIPTION:	The primary focus of the Emergency Vehicle Operator- Heavy (EVO-H) is the safe operation of heavy or large emergency vehicles over 26,000 lbs GVW with special operating requirements (airbrakes, medium or heavy-duty chassis) used for patient care and/or transport.

Table 13-1: Required Criteria

TRAINING:
SEE NOTE 1
	Completion of the following courses/curricula:
	1. ICS-100: Introduction to ICS.
	2. IS-700.A: NIMS, An Introduction.
	3. IS-800.B: NRF, An Introduction.
	4. HazMat Awareness Training or equivalent basic instruction consistent with:
	    a. the hazards anticipated to be present, or present at the scene
	    b. the probable impact of those hazards, based upon the mission role of the individual
	    c. use of the personal protective equipment consistent with "Guidance on Emergency Responder Personal Protective Equipment (PPE) for Response to CBRN Terrorism Incidents," Dept of HHS, Centers for Disease Control and Prevention, National Institute for Occupational Safety and Health (June 2008).
	5. CEVO or equivalent.
	6. DDC4 or equivalent.

EXPERIENCE:	1. Ongoing, active participation with an EMS-providing entity, organization, or agency. 2. Demonstrate basic competency of vehicle operation.
LICENSING:	Valid driver's license with appropriate endorsements if required by licensing state.
COMMENTS:	**Note 1:** Per NIMS compliance at the time of publication, ICS and IS training courses are listed. Equivalent courses must meet the NIMS Five-Year Training Plan. As NIMS compliance requirements change, the requirements in this document will change to match them.

Table 13-2: Recommended Criteria

EXPERIENCE:	2 years minimum driving experience, plus a minimum of 1 year EVO and 1 year EVO-H experience.

PHYSICAL/ MEDICAL FITNESS:	1. Individuals must be healthy enough to function under field conditions, which may include some or all of the following: • 12-hour shifts, austere conditions (possibly no showers, housing in tents, portable toilets). • Extreme weather conditions (long exposure to heat and humidity, lack of air conditioning, extreme cold, wet environments). • Long periods of standing. 2. Individuals should not require personal medications that require refrigeration. 3. Individuals should not have any physical conditions, impairments, or restrictions that would preclude them from participating in the moving and lifting of patients and/or equipment and supplies. 4. Immunizations: Refer to immunization recommendations for emergency responders by Centers for Disease Control, including: • Td toxoid or Tdap. Receipt of primary series and booster within the past 10 years. • Completion of Hepatitis B Vaccination Series OR completion of a waiver of liability.

14. EMS Physician	
DESCRIPTION:	The primary purpose of the EMS Physician is to ensure quality patient care and provide medical oversight of EMS resources within an established command and control system during an incident response. The EMS Physician: 1. Is a licensed physician who possesses the education and experience in areas of medicine and out-of-hospital care commensurate with the patient care mission. 2. Primary responsibilities include the development and initiation of EMS protocols, oversight of EMS resource allocation, appropriate triage, treatment, handling, and transportation of victims. 3. Has the authority over all patient care and clinical aspects of the EMS service.

Table 14-1: Required Criteria

EDUCATION:	Graduate of an accredited medical school and completion of an accredited residency program.

TRAINING:	Completion of the following courses/curricula:
	
	 1. ICS-100: Introduction to ICS.
	
	 2. ICS-200: Basic ICS.
	
	 3. ICS-300: Intermediate ICS.
	
	 4. IS-700.A: NIMS, An Introduction.
	
	 5. IS-800.B: NRF, An Introduction.
	
	 6. HazMat Awareness Training or equivalent basic instruction consistent with:
	
	    a. the hazards anticipated to be present, or present at the scene
	
	    b. the probable impact of those hazards, based upon the mission role of the individual
	
	    c. use of the personal protective equipment consistent with "Guidance on Emergency Responder Personal Protective Equipment (PPE) for Response to CBRN Terrorism Incidents," Dept of HHS, Centers for Disease Control and Prevention, National Institute for Occupational Safety and Health (June 2008).
	
	 7. Pre-deployment briefing on Federal, State, and/or local MCI and disaster plans and applicable EMS laws and regulations for area to which the disaster response/resources have been directed.

EXPERIENCE:	1. Minimum of 2 years experience or training in out-of-hospital emergency care of the acutely ill or injured patient. 2. Knowledge of Federal, State, and local MCI disaster plans. 3. Actively provides medical direction to an EMS service.
CERTIFICATION:	Current DEA registration.
LICENSING:	Active status of legal authority to function as a physician granted by a state, the District of Columbia, or U.S. territory.

Table 14-2: Recommended Criteria

EDUCATION:	Post-graduate education in emergency medicine (or comparable specialty).
TRAINING:	Completion of the following courses/curricula: 1. Base Station Course or equivalent. 2. Nationally or state recognized EMS Medical Director Course or Curriculum. 3. Completion of 8 hours annually of Category 1 Continuing Medical Education (CME) based on EMS related content.
CERTIFICATION:	1. Active status of legal authority to function as an EMS Physician, EMS Medical Director, or equivalent granted by a state, the District of Columbia, or U.S. territory. 2. Board certification or board-eligible in emergency medicine.

PHYSICAL/ MEDICAL FITNESS:	1. Individuals must be healthy enough to function under field conditions, which may include some or all of the following:
	  • 12-hour shifts, austere conditions (possibly no showers, housing in tents, portable toilets).
	  • Extreme weather conditions (long exposure to heat and humidity, lack of air conditioning, extreme cold, wet environments).
	  • Long periods of standing.
	2. Individuals should not require personal medications that require refrigeration.
	3. Individuals should not have any physical conditions, impairments, or restrictions that would preclude them from participating in the moving and lifting of patients and/or equipment and supplies.
	4. Immunizations:
	Refer to immunization recommendations for emergency responders by Centers for Disease Control, including:
	  • Td toxoid or Tdap. Receipt of primary series and booster within the past 10 years.
	  • Completion of Hepatitis B Vaccination Series OR completion of a waiver of liability.

15. Medical Supply Coordinator	
DESCRIPTION:	The primary focus of the Medical Supply Coordinator is to acquire and maintain control of appropriate medical equipment and supplies for units assigned to the medical group. The Medical Supply Coordinator coordinates with logistics section of ICS to accomplish medical resupply and ensures distribution to EMS treatment and triage units.

Table 15-1: Required Criteria

EDUCATION:	Completion of state-approved First Responder or EMR program based on NHTSA National Standard Curriculum.

TRAINING: **SEE NOTE 1**	Completion of the following courses/curricula:
	 1. ICS-100: Introduction to ICS.
	 2. ICS-200: Basic ICS.
	 3. IS-700.A: NIMS, An Introduction.
	 4. IS-800.B: NRF, An Introduction.
	 5. HazMat Awareness Training or equivalent basic instruction consistent with:
	     a. the hazards anticipated to be present, or present at the scene
	     b. the probable impact of those hazards, based upon the mission role of the individual
	     c. use of the personal protective equipment consistent with "Guidance on Emergency Responder Personal Protective Equipment (PPE) for Response to CBRN Terrorism Incidents," Dept of HHS, Centers for Disease Control and Prevention, National Institute for Occupational Safety and Health (June 2008).

EXPERIENCE:	Ongoing, active participation with an EMS-providing entity, organization, or agency.
LICENSING:	Active status of legal authority to function at the minimum of First Responder or EMR granted by a state, the District of Columbia, or U.S. territory.
COMMENTS:	**Note 1:** Per NIMS compliance at the time of publication, ICS and IS training courses are listed. Equivalent courses must meet the NIMS Five-Year Training Plan. As NIMS compliance requirements change, the requirements in this document will change to match them.

Table 15-2: Recommended Criteria

EDUCATION:	Successful completion of the minimum terminal learning objectives for EMR as defined by NHTSA National EMS Education Standards. See Note 1.
TRAINING:	Completion of the following courses/curricula: 1. ICS-300: Intermediate ICS. 2. Ongoing training in the management and care of patients involved in a MCI.

PHYSICAL/ MEDICAL FITNESS:	1. Individuals must be healthy enough to function under field conditions, which may include some or all of the following: • 12-hour shifts, austere conditions (possibly no showers, housing in tents, portable toilets). • Extreme weather conditions (long exposure to heat and humidity, lack of air conditioning, extreme cold, wet environments). • Long periods of standing. 2. Individuals should not require personal medications that require refrigeration. 3. Individuals should not have any physical conditions, impairments, or restrictions that would preclude them from participating in the moving and lifting of patients and/or equipment and supplies. 4. Immunizations: Refer to immunization recommendations for emergency responders by Centers for Disease Control, including: • Td toxoid or Tdap. Receipt of primary series and booster within the past 10 years. • Completion of Hepatitis B Vaccination Series OR completion of a waiver of liability.
COMMENTS:	**Note 1:** NHTSA National EMS Education Standards are a component of the EMS Education Agenda for the Future: A System Approach, a comprehensive plan for a national EMS education system. The State equivalent to EMRs, EMTs, Advanced EMTs and paramedics are expected to transition to these educational standards as they are implemented.

16. Paramedic	
DESCRIPTION:	The primary focus of the paramedic is to provide emergency care based on an advanced assessment and the formulation of a field impression, including basic and advanced skills focusing on the acute management and transportation of the broad range of patients who access the emergency medical system. The paramedic: 1. Possesses the education and experience in areas of medicine and pre-hospital care commensurate with the patient care mission. 2. Skills include triage, assessment, and ongoing monitoring capabilities as well as invasive and pharmacological interventions to reduce the morbidity and mortality associated with acute out-of-hospital medical and traumatic emergencies. 3. Provides care designed to minimize secondary injury and provide comfort to the patient and family while transporting the patient to an appropriate health care facility. Paramedic is the minimum licensure level required for the full range of advanced out-of-hospital care.

Table 16-1: Required Criteria

EDUCATION:	Completion of a state-approved paramedic program based on NHTSA National Standard Curriculum.

TRAINING:
SEE NOTE 1
	Completion of the following courses/curricula:
	
	1. ICS-100: Introduction to ICS.
	
	2. IS-700.A: NIMS, An Introduction.
	
	3. IS-800.B: NRF, An Introduction.
	
	4. HazMat Awareness Training or equivalent basic instruction consistent with:
	
	   a. the hazards anticipated to be present, or present at the scene
	
	   b. the probable impact of those hazards, based upon the mission role of the individual
	
	   c. use of the personal protective equipment consistent with "Guidance on Emergency Responder Personal Protective Equipment (PPE) for Response to CBRN Terrorism Incidents," Dept of HHS, Centers for Disease Control and Prevention, National Institute for Occupational Safety and Health (June 2008).

EXPERIENCE:	Ongoing, active participation with an EMS-providing entity, organization, or agency.
CERTIFICATION:	Successful completion of a state-approved program at this level or NREMT certification at this level.
LICENSING:	Active status of legal authority to function as a paramedic granted by a state, the District of Columbia, or U.S. territory.

COMMENTS:	**Note 1:** Per NIMS compliance at the time of publication, ICS and IS training courses are listed. Equivalent courses must meet the NIMS Five-Year Training Plan. As NIMS compliance requirements change, the requirements in this document will change to match them.
	Note 2: The personnel descriptions contained in this document are based upon the guidelines contained in the National EMS Scope of Practice Model document, which can be found at www.ems.gov.

Table 16-2: Recommended Criteria

EDUCATION:	Successful completion of the minimal terminal learning objectives for paramedic as defined by NHSTA National EMS Education Standards. See Note 1.
TRAINING:	Completion of the following courses/curricula: 1. ICS 200: Basic ICS. 1. Ongoing training in the management and care of patients involved in a MCI.

PHYSICAL/ MEDICAL FITNESS:	1. Individuals must be healthy enough to function under field conditions, which may include some or all of the following:
	  • 12-hour shifts, austere conditions (possibly no showers, housing in tents, portable toilets).
	  • Extreme weather conditions (long exposure to heat and humidity, lack of air conditioning, extreme cold, wet environments).
	  • Long periods of standing.
	2. Individuals should not require personal medications that require refrigeration.
	3. Individuals should not have any physical conditions, impairments, or restrictions that would preclude them from participating in the moving and lifting of patients and/or equipment and supplies.
	4. Immunizations:
	Refer to immunization recommendations for emergency responders by Centers for Disease Control, including:
	  • Td toxoid or Tdap. Receipt of primary series and booster within the past 10 years.
	  • Completion of Hepatitis B Vaccination Series OR completion of a waiver of liability.

COMMENTS:	**Note 1:** NHTSA National EMS Education Standards are a component of the EMS Education Agenda for the Future: A System Approach, a comprehensive plan for a national EMS education system. The State equivalent to EMRs, EMTs, Advanced EMTs and paramedics are expected to transition to these educational standards as they are implemented.

www.ingramcontent.com/pod-product-compliance
Lightning Source LLC
Chambersburg PA
CBHW080733290526
45790CB00008B/3179